FOR CONNIE
COME + DISCOVER
PORTSMOUTH
Marianne Young

PORTSMOUTH LOOKING UP!

*a unique walking tour
of our historic downtown*

Photography by Marianne Pernold Young

Portsmouth Looking Up! books are available at special quantity discounts
for bulk purchases for sales promotions, premiums, fund-raising and educational needs.

Pernold Publishing

Marianne Pernold Young
579 Sagamore Ave, Unit 19
Portsmouth, NH 03801
portsmouthlookingup.com

ISBN 978-1-45-7-2170-7

Portsmouth Looking Up! – A Unique Walking Tour of Our Historic Downtown

HISTORY OF PORTSMOUTH, NEW HAMPSHIRE

New England grew inland from the sea. Portsmouth remains New Hampshire's only seaport, the historical and cultural hub of the smallest coastline in America. Established in 1623, settled in 1630, Portsmouth's heyday as a world trade center peaked soon after the American Revolution. The city's economy rose and fell as the tide of war impacted shipbuilding at the Portsmouth Naval Shipyard across the fast-flowing Piscataqua River in Kittery, Maine. As American industrial cities grew, tourists were drawn to the preserved colonial mansions of "The Old Town by the Sea" and to the rocky Isles of Shoals nearby. A cultural renaissance in the second half of the 20th century transformed Portsmouth into a heritage destination now considered among the most beautiful "walkable" small cities in the nation.

SeacoastNH.com

INTRODUCTION & HOW TO USE THIS BOOK

Portsmouth Looking Up! is intended to help the reader discover the architectural legacy of Portsmouth, New Hampshire while gaining an appreciation of the dedication and effort that have preserved these landmarks for present and future generations. Using the photo images and map, see how many of these elements of architecture, art and artifact you can identify through the images and caption clues. Certainly, you will discover new elements on your own. For your walking tour, each image is numbered and keyed to the map located on the last page. Look up, enjoy the tour, and gain a greater appreciation and understanding of the beauty and history of the port city we call home.

Oh, the rewards of *Looking Up!*

The beautiful architectural details of this Federal-style building may escape the notice of former patrons and current visitors since the main entrance is located in a modern connector linking it to an adjoining Federal house. Note the hip roofs of both older structures and the marble course that runs around the building above the double-columned doorways.

A former parish house for a landmark downtown church, this building continues to offer shelter and sustenance to those in need. If you get a corner red light, take a moment to notice the architectural details and consider volunteering here.

It's worth walking a few blocks from Market Square and stroll down this street with its beautifully appointed homes. The detail pictured is from a house built by B. F. Webster, a leading late 19th century builder. It's hard to absorb all the details, but do note the slate mansard roof, stately corner pilasters and the gorgeous central bay with this exquisitely detailed window.

We have Woodbury Langdon and Frank Jones to thank for this monument to the Colonial Revival period. Originally Langdon's home, it was converted to a hotel by Jones in 1870. When the building burned in 1884, the dining room with its leather ceiling was saved and can be seen in the current restaurant. Standing between its stately golden lions, look up to see the ornate medallions and sculptured masks.

Built in 1814, this beautiful Federal-style house was later enhanced by Colonial Revival elements including this distinctive Palladian window. Note the unusual *fleur de lis* design on the decorative keystone. Captain Thomas Shaw and his brother Abraham were wealthy merchants and funded this building using privateering profits accrued during the War of 1812.

Reflective of the architecture of the '50s, with additions in '60s and '70s, this modern structure has always been a bank, although the name has changed several times. Propped on a corner without regard to surrounding historical styles, this utilitarian building honors its presence in a port city with this tide clock. Whether sailor, shipbuilder or beachcomber, the tides continue to rule the activities of those privileged to call this city home.

This imposing granite structure once served as a federal

building housing offices of the U. S. Postal Service, IRS,

FBI and Social Security; all of which moved many years

ago to a modern structure on Daniel Street. The building's

interior vestibule clearly reflects the formality of its original

function – as does the Italian *palazzo* style exterior.

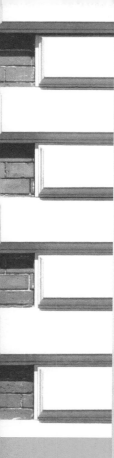

Currently this building houses food and fashion on the ground floor with offices and apartments above. These decorative copper window caps were perhaps more in keeping with its former formal functions as a bank and City Hall. What then was considered gaudy is today seen as a beautiful decorative element on an otherwise plain corner building.

This early Federal-style church building no longer has its bell tower. The extended Italianate eaves pictured here were added circa 1860. However, time travelers from the past would still recognize it by the three semi-circular arched doors below three similarly designed windows. It continues to draw the faithful for Saturday services.

If you were escorted into this police station before it was converted to its current use, you would have been less interested in its Richardsonian Romanesque architectural details than in avoiding an extended stay. Famed Boston architect H. H. Richardson is responsible for this style's name which can be identified by the asymmetrical façade, projecting bays and contrasting stone trim. This building's architect, Ralph Adams Cram, was famous for his Gothic Revival work.

Follow your nose to this popular spot and take a moment to look up and admire this whimsical metal portrait of Ceres, created by our local blacksmith. Once a storage area for an adjoining inn, it has become a favorite eating and meeting place for Portsmouth locals.

On this quiet street is a modern rooftop solarium, adorned with intricate ironwork. The building itself fronts on a street running perpendicular to this one. Without looking up towards the back of the building, this gorgeous contemporary addition would be missed entirely.

Members of the Sheafe family were politicians, merchants and ship captains who brought much to Portsmouth including (inadvertently) an epidemic of yellow fever in 1798 that proved fatal to 55 city residents. Along the short street bearing their name, you will find these architectural details on a private home.

In Portsmouth, quiet streets often hold hidden treasures:

beautiful ironwork staircases, pocket gardens, balconies

and – on this house – a rustic chimney adorned with

cast concrete masks.

This mid-19th century brick Italianate style building was a high

school before becoming Portsmouth's City Hall. Today, this

building provides office space for a variety of businesses.

Below the detailed wood trim is a trio of rounded windows.

The beautiful classic portico is supported by Tuscan columns.

Squeezed against the gabled end of its neighbor, this wooden duplex has two center doors capped by this colorful hood and scrolled brackets. The building's former tenants included a used book store, a beauty salon and – most memorably – Emilio's.

Another cornerstone in downtown Portsmouth is this Federal-style building and its easily identifiable Palladian window crowned by a stucco arch and louvered fan. Originally it was the customs house and post office, as well as a meeting place for various organizations. Ironically, today it faces its contemporary counterpart.

The first floor of this flat-roofed late 19th century commercial building has been occupied by a variety of restaurants serving specialty cuisines, from Chinese to Mexican. The frieze with the name "J. B. PAHLS" on the central parapet acknowledges the structure's original builder and owner, an early purveyor of baked goods.

This faded wall of advertising history would be missed by most. Left alone, it represents a graphic timeline of the many merchants who have chosen this location for their business. Currently a store featuring artful glassware, this address has been a meat and provisions market, a coal and appliance store and even a karate studio! It is a credit to the building's owner that this ephemera has been preserved rather than removed.

This peeling "nod to the past" decorative detail adorns the last building in this brick Federal row block that welcomes all who enter Portsmouth along the working waterfront. This row, noted for the distinctive stepped firewalls rising between the buildings, has been modified significantly at the storefront level reflecting changing styles and functions. Hugging the southern corner, this storefront once was home to the Italian Meat and Provision Cooperative and frequented by many residents of the old North End before it was razed in 1969.

Today they line up at the front door of this Italianate brick building for a microbrew, and few might notice the curved copper cornices above its windows. In its heyday, this dry goods store held sway over its lesser neighbors. Oh, for the good old days when shopping downtown was the rule, not the exception. In the '80s it was a popular shopping arcade.

Built in 1780 in one of Portsmouth's picturesque brick row blocks, this building was later embellished by high Victorian classical touches in 1880 (hence the two dates on the façade). Guarding the entrance to a popular connecting alley, it was once a popular dry goods store that later became an equally well-known department store. Both bore the owner's name: Kimball.

This street was initially named Graffort's Lane after Bridgit Graffort donated the land to the town. However, in 1813 the town fathers renamed the street after her first husband. It is one of several routes from the bustling waterfront to the center of town. Along this street you will find a blend of old and modern architecture of varying distinction and building materials. Looking up from an iconic eating spot, you will notice this contemporary adornment on its chimney.

Continuing along the former Graffort's Lane, one approaches
Market Square, the community hub of Portsmouth. Looking up
the side of this building you can view the beautiful detailed
brickwork adorning the upper façade. Around the corner was
once home to Teddy's Lunch in the '80s, Café Brioche in
the '90s and is now a popular café.

The site of Portsmouth's financial center since 1703, this stately structure maintained its fiduciary purpose from 1803 until the late 20th century overseeing the financial affairs of Portsmouth families and businesses. Renovated in 1903, it contains neo-classical and *Beaux-Arts* elements – different styles unique to the two banks that once conducted business here. Today, allow the strains of Celtic music to entice you indoors to view handsome interior woodwork and – overhead – a dramatic stained glass dome.

This Federal-style building, noted for its curved parapet and composite pilasters, is an architectural icon of downtown Portsmouth. Built in 1805, it has known only two occupants. First, the New Hampshire Fire & Marine Insurance Company and, since 1823, the Portsmouth Athenæum. Here is preserved the history of Portsmouth and the Seacoast region, where its keeper and proprietors keep watch over its art, archives and library.

Designed by Portsmouth architect William Ashe, this Romanesque building built in the 1890's has enjoyed tenants from bankers to bakeries and toys to trinkets. Admire these *terracotta* rosettes in the front gables and be sure to inspect the wrought ironwork on the side of the building.

Built in 1937, this three-bay block has a concrete façade that incorporates the above design. One of two downtown buildings in the Art Deco style, it has been home to many offices and shops. Over the years, you might have had your hair cut, lunched on pizza, or bought your "smokes" or bus tickets at one of its three storefronts. Some may even recall catching matinees at the old theater.

As film processing gave way to digitization, this block rose from the rubble to settle comfortably into the streetscape as the new kid on the block. From this oculus, its residents have a great view of Market Square. At street level, vistors may enjoy delicious food and drink or purchase their latest book.

This large-scale structure in the Romanesque style with Gothic touches and mansard roof, was built for beer baron Frank Jones in 1878. The style reflects Portsmouth's economic transition from a shipbuilding community to a thriving commercial center. Note the second floor balcony from which occupants could watch the numerous parades of the time.

Since the American Revolution, Portsmouth has been a vital

community of the arts. Designed by Boston architect Arthur

Vinal, this building was a notable theater and movie house.

It features these fascinating faces above the pillars of the Gothic

arch. At one time the entrance to a burlesque revue, this block

is now home to professional offices and retail businesses.

Once the address of Portsmouth's prison, and in a later incarnation a lecture and concert hall, this edifice may not be fancy on the outside, but its interior has been painstakingly restored and is simply striking! Designated an "American Treasure" by the National Park Service, this institution is one of Portsmouth's foremost cultural destinations.

Previously a fine hotel with a preferred corner location, this mansard style brick building was built after the Civil War and is a beautiful and rare New Hampshire example of Old Boston style row houses with their bowed fronts on either side of a central entry. Purchase a piece of jewelry on one side and then run – don't walk – to the other store.

This business block might seem out of place in downtown Portsmouth, yet during the 1930's, Art Deco style was all the rage. This building provides a good example of the period with its stepped piers and Arabesque patterns. Though unremarkable at street level, one must look up to take in the details of this unique example of commercial architecture.

A refreshing change from the ubiquitous red brick of

Portsmouth, this yellow brick three-story building is now

a residence for some who once attended high school here.

Named for the famous Civil War admiral who declared

"damn the torpedoes!", this building was saved from the

demolition ball in 1980.

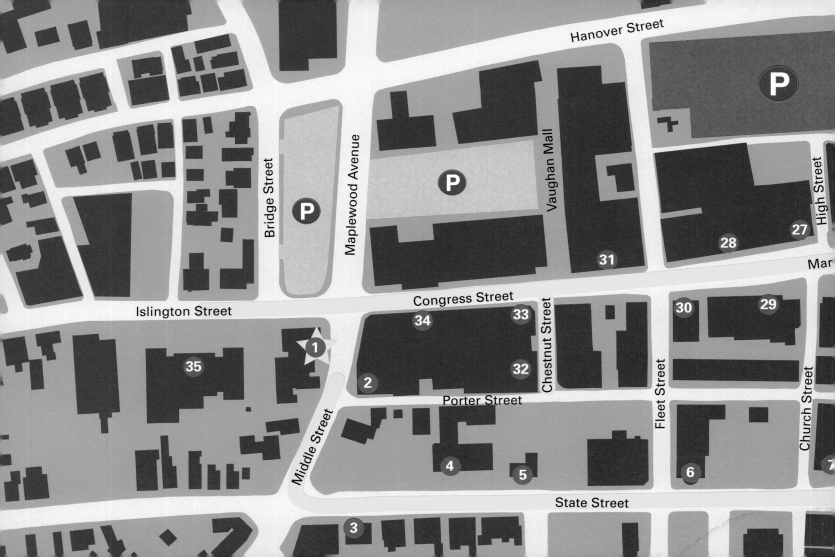

CREDITS

Design/Editing

Boyd Morrison & Cindy Tuttle **Gamble Design** LLC Portsmouth, NH
whose creativity, cartography and design expertise gave this book its form

Copy

Carolyn Marvin **Portsmouth Athenæum** Portsmouth, NH
whose enthusiasm and historical knowledge added a new dimension

Contributors

J. Dennis Robinson, Bob Thoresen, Sam Jarvis, Norm Kent, James McCarty
and many others for their terrific stories, suggestions and assistance

> **image** Seal of the State of New Hampshire 22-26 Market Street (26)